THREE PATHS TO A DECENT LIFE

Also by Leslie Scrase:

Days in the Sun (children's stories, with Jean Head)
In Travellings Often
Booklet on Anglican/Methodist Conversations
Some Sussex and Surrey Scrases
Diamond Parents
The Sunlight Glances Through (poetry)
Some Ancestors of Humanism
An Evacuee
Conversations (on Matthew's Gospel)
             between an Atheist and a Christian
A Prized Pupil!
A Reluctant Seaman
The Game Goes On (poetry)
It's Another World
A Talented Bureaucrat
Town Mouse and Country Mouse (nature diary)
More from the Country Mouse (nature diary)
Kenneth and Bob (children's story)
Letting off Steam (short essays)
Scribblings of an old romantic (poems)
Happy Endings (short stories)
An Unbeliever's Guide to the Bible
The Four Gospels Through an Outside Window
                  – A Commentary
Autobiography of a Blockhead (poetry)
Postscript (poetry)
Belief, Unbelief, Ethics and Life
Driven Crazy – My Life with Cars & Other Vehicles
Infamous Last Words (poetry)
Footprints in the Sand (poetry)
A Late Harvest (poetry)
Coping With Death (4th Edition)
An Unknown Poet Sings
Jesus for a Secular Age?

THREE
PATHS TO A
DECENT LIFE

Dismantling the teaching of St. Paul
Sequel to *Jesus for a Secular Age?*

Leslie Scrase

UNITED WRITERS
Cornwall

UNITED WRITERS PUBLICATIONS LTD
Ailsa, Castle Gate, Penzance, Cornwall.
www.unitedwriters.co.uk

British Library Cataloguing in Publication Data:
A catalogue record for this book is
available from the British Library.

ISBN 9781852002145

Printed and bound in Great Britain by
United Writers Publications Ltd.,
Cornwall.

To my children
Richard, Andrew, Jean and Christine.

Acknowledgements

The manuscript of this small book came from three dying typewriters and a disastrous failed attempt to master a word processor. I'm so grateful to Malcolm Sheppard of United Writers for turning perhaps my worst ever original into this book for me.

Contents

(Most Biblical quotations are from the New English Bible.)

*Many persons strive for high ideals
and everywhere life is full of heroism.*
Max Ehrmann.

*'Your letters remain. . .
we, pottering among the foothills
of their logic, find ourselves staring
across deep crevices at conclusions
                        at which
the living Jesus would not willingly
                have arrived.'*
R.S. Thomas.

Preface

When we are young children we are too busy actually living to give any thought to the meaning of life or to ask what it means to live life well. And even in our teens, when we are beginning to have to face questions about what we are going to do with our lives; what our hopes and ambitions are; I still don't think most of us give much thought to life itself – to the question of what it is all about. We just face the problems we have to face and get on with dealing with them.

How are we going to earn a living? Do we want to live alone or with a partner? Is there one special partner who knocks us for six and bowls us over? Where on earth are we going to manage to find to live? Can we afford to buy our own home or do we have to rent? Do we want/can we afford children?

All those practical things dominate our thinking. As a result, we never step back and look at life, at what it is all about. Yet, if we were asked, I think that most of us would say that we want to live our lives as well as we can. Without making too much fuss about it, that is what we want to do. And on the whole, I think that most of us succeed.

Over the course of my lifetime I have conducted something over 6,000 funerals which means that I have visited over 6,000 homes. Those homes have been very varied but my general impression has always been that most of us make a pretty good job of living warm, welcoming, friendly, loving, companionable lives.

In this country, if we wanted guidance on how to live well, we would traditionally have turned to Christianity, to the churches and to the Bible. Jesus would have been our guide. In my recent book about Jesus (*Jesus for a Secular Age?*), I have shown that he still has valuable things to say.

Anybody who still turns to Christianity will soon find that s/he is confronted by St. Paul. He was one of the first to try to work out the significance of Jesus. But he did so without ever having known Jesus and without having access to the four gospels. None of those had been written when Paul was working and writing his letters.

In my book about Jesus, I focussed on his ministry and his teaching. Paul didn't. He focussed almost exclusively on the death and resurrection. He believed that without faith in what Jesus tried to achieve through his death and resurrection, a good life is impossible, and the rewards associated with it are impossible too.

In this book I hope to show that he was wrong, and to show how much simpler life really is.

I have tried very hard to make dry-as-dust subjects readable and complex subjects reasonably straightforward. I hope that 1 have made it possible for readers to travel with me.

My goal has been to try to define what I mean by living a good life. What does it mean to live well?

After wrestling with the apostle Paul I find that by being

very selective, I can agree with him about two fundamental foundations of a good life. In my final two chapters I hope that I have shown that, in essence, the good life is something very simple. Knowing what it is is one thing. Actually living it is another. For many of us there will be hiccoughs along the way – I've had my own – but my conviction is that in the end, most of us manage to make a pretty good job of living our lives to the best of our abilities.

Chapter 1

Paul

When John the Baptist died, a few of his disciples continued to promulgate his teachings. As a result a small sect survived for a number of *centuries* before finally dying out.

When Jesus died, quite a lot of his disciples did the same – as Paul's letters demonstrate. Paul didn't think much of most of them. Nor was he altogether happy with the brand of Christianity they offered. (Yes. There were different brands right from the start.) But in spite of all those disciples, it is possible that Christianity would have gone the same way as the sect of John the Baptist – without Paul.

Paul changed everything. There are similarities between him and John Wesley in the eighteenth century. Both were tireless travellers. Both had a real gift for organisation. And both of them took their message to people who had no worthwhile religion or philosophy to follow. Wesley created the Methodist branch of the Christian Church. Paul was largely responsible for the creation and establishment of the Christian Church itself. Neither of them did their work alone but each of them was the stand-out religionist of his time.

Paul was more important for the establishment of the

Christian church than any of the remaining eleven apostles chosen by Jesus – more important than all of them put together. It is even arguable that he was more important than Jesus himself, although no Christian will thank me for saying so.

But Jesus never seemed to have a real plan. He never seemed to know what he was aiming for. There *was* one brief moment when he talked about creating his church but he provided no blue-print, gave no guidance as to what that church should look like.

It was Paul who used the Jewish synagogues as a model on which to base the early organisation of the church. It was Paul who gave a hierarchical structure to the local church he set up. It was Paul who took Christianity away from Judaism and gave it to non-Jews, to people who had no significant religion of their own. It was Paul who first began to formulate a theology from which, much later, came the Christian creeds.

He was a tireless traveller and missionary. He was an excellent organiser. And although he was not a systematic thinker, he *was* a real thinker whose thinking will demand our attention.

So who was he?

Born in Tarsus, he was a Jew of the Dispersion, not a Palestinian Jew. His upbringing will have focussed on the synagogue, not on the temple in Jerusalem. In addition to being a Jew he was also a Roman citizen. That was to become significant when he was finally arrested and condemned to death. Using his citizenship, he appealed against his sentence to Caesar and was sent to Rome where the sentence was upheld and he was put to death.

But in his early life he was a more than devout Jew,

passionate about his religion and appalled at the new sect of followers of Jesus. He went to Palestine, made himself known to the Jewish leaders and became, with their authority, a persecutor of the Christians. He was zealous and an extremist. Most Jewish leaders would probably have been content to leave Christianity to wither away. Paul believed that it must be destroyed.

And then he had a momentous conversion experience when he was travelling to Damascus. It is described in the Acts of the Apostles, Chapter 9. Paul being Paul, you would not expect anything to be done by halves. From being a persecutor of Christians, in a very short space of time he became a leading promoter of the new religion.

He went back to Jerusalem and got to know some of the Christian leaders, including Peter the apostle. I suspect that once they had got over their initial suspicions of him they found him a pretty uncomfortable companion. Paul was a man who always believed that he was right. His understanding of Jesus was superior to that of those who had known Jesus. He knew better even than those who had been chosen by Jesus. His interpretation of Christianity and of the way Christianity should grow and develop and be taught was the only possible correct interpretation.

He must have been a real pain in the neck. Zealots of any kind are not that easy to live with. When he suggested that he should carry Christianity to that part of the world from which he came, the rest of them were probably only too glad to authorise him and to see the back of him.

Since he had no specific qualifications, nothing on paper that could demonstrate his authority as a promoter of the faith, and since there had been no ordination ceremony to underpin his authority, Paul always had to lay claim to his authority himself. His letters contain a series of those claims – some of them really went over the top. In Romans, the first of the letters in the New Testament, he was fairly restrained. He wrote to say that he was:

'a servant of Jesus Christ
an apostle by God's call and
set apart for the service of the Gospel.'

Through Jesus (Jesus himself – not through the apostles note); through Jesus 'I received the privilege of a commission to lead men in all nations to faith and obedience (in and to) Jesus.'

'I am under obligation to Greek and non-Greek, to learned and simple.'

'God's way starts in faith and ends in faith.'

That last sentence is crucial.

Religion is not a matter of knowledge or fact. It is a matter of belief – faith. Either we believe or we do not believe. Our relationship with religion is as simple as that.

In this book I propose to look at some of Paul's teaching again through those of his letters that were published in the New Testament. Through that publication they became 'Holy Scripture', 'the Word of God'. Some parts of them are sublime. Other parts of them are about as awful as anything you will ever meet. If there really is a God, I sincerely hope that he/she/it is as far removed as possible from some of the contents of Paul's letters. They really do make grim reading at times.

And oddly enough, although they carry that designation 'Holy Scripture' and 'the Word of God' parts of the Christian church have turned their back on parts of Paul's teaching and gone against it completely – as we shall see.

Chapter 2

Paul: A Child of His Time

We are all of us children of our own time. We imbibe the ideas, standards and morals of our own time. Paul was no exception. He had ideas which seem very strange to us – strange and also plain wrong. That wouldn't matter except that Christians incorporated his letters into the New Testament and treated them as Scripture – the Word of God. Because of that, ideas which now seem just strange and dated have caused a great deal of harm, and to a degree they still do. Paul is not to blame for that. He was only a man, after all. But the church is to blame.

It is to blame because it often hangs onto old and harmful ideas long after the rest of us have discarded them. As Richard Holloway put it when he was Bishop of Edinburgh, 'The impetus for social reforms usually happens with the Church right at the back of the process.'

Paul's ideas of sex and marriage are very strange. They probably seemed strange in his own time. He himself was a bachelor and a celibate bachelor at that. Perhaps his ideas were influenced by his belief that the end time was very near and that it might well come within his own life-time. Crackpots have often shared his view, thinking the end would come in their own lifetimes. With the coming of global warming perhaps those ideas are not quite as crackpot as they were. But Paul's ideas of sex and marriage certainly were.

First of all, he was virulent in his hatred of same sex relationships, echoing views expressed in the Old Testament.

I must confess that I dislike the sexual elements of same-sex relationships. But as long as they are genuinely consensual between adults I cannot see that anyone has any right to interfere. Similarly, I do not like people parading their sexuality, although I can understand why the LGB community has felt the need to do so. But my own dislikes and reservations are as nothing compared with the vitriol of Paul.

Most of the same sex relationships of which he would have been aware would have been between men and men and between men and boys. Those between men and boys did need to be called into question. They still do.

But his virulence was all embracing and the church has still not freed itself from his vile opinions.

Just now I quoted Bishop (as he was then) Richard Holloway. He was present at the Lambeth Conference of 1998 which reaffirmed 'Christianity's traditional rejection of same-sex relationships' and 'evinced a degree of hatred of homosexuals that many observers found frightening'. 'Speaker after speaker quoted the Bible as though it was the final word on a complex subject so that no further thinking needed to be done.' (See his book *Godless Morality*).

But Paul's ideas of 'ordinary' sex and marriage were very strange too. He urged people to follow his celibate example and only to marry if they couldn't control their sexual appetites. As a result of Paul's attitude there came a time when the Roman Catholic church decided to insist that all the clergy should be celibate. It was a disastrous decision.

There were Popes who had a number of children out of wedlock and, of course, the same was true of many of the ordinary clergy. It makes you wonder at the lack of respect for the women concerned and also at the cruelty shown towards 'illegitimate' children for so long.

But the insistence on celibacy has had far more serious outcomes than papal or clergy children. In our own time we have seen scandal after scandal concerning men of the church and their behaviour towards children in their care. This kind of scandal is not restricted to the church or to Christians but there can be no doubt that the failure of the celibacy ideal has led to serious damage to a host of children. And this evil has been compounded by a conspiracy of silence in which the church has tried to hide the scale of the evil and to protect its own.

But there is a wider downside to this idea that clergy should be celibate. It means that Roman Catholic clergy have no experience of marriage, no experience of the deepest of human relationships. As a result, they are in no position to advise other people about their relationships.

Paul believed that the only reason for marriage was to avoid immorality. 'Better to marry than to burn with desire.' But 'those who marry will have pain and grief in this bodily life.' In spite of the magnificent passage on love in his letter to the Corinthians, a passage which so many people use at their weddings, Paul seems to have had no idea that marriage could involve such love. In all that he had to say about marriage there seemed to be no element of personal feeling at all. Paul certainly had no concept of romantic love

18

or mutual attraction. He had no idea of how wonderful marriage can be when two well-matched people develop over a period of many years a relationship which is unsurpassable.

(I should perhaps add that in my own thinking marriage and 'partnership' are indistinguishable. For me, lasting partnerships are simply marriages without the preliminary of a ceremony.)

In all that Paul has to say about marriage there is no reference to children. Perhaps, if the end of the world is just around the corner, children are felt to be unnecessary. But Paul seems to have had no idea at all of marriage as the foundation of family life – of all the love and richness that children can bring, or of an ever growing circle of love and affection.

In some marriages children seem to be the be-all and end-all of married life. They are the heart and soul of the marriage. In others, they are more like the cream-icing on the cake. Either way they can be an inexpressibly valuable part of marriage. Having a family can be a wonderful enrichment to life and to marriage. But Paul seems to have none of the affection Jesus had for children. For him it was not so much a case of 'Children should be seen and not heard' as 'out of sight and out of mind'.

When Paul wrote about marriage he expressed his attitude towards women as forcibly as he expressed all his opinions. I don't think many women would be very happy with his views.

'The man is the head of the woman' so 'wives be subject to your husbands. Women must be subject to their husbands in everything.' A woman 'must see to it that she pays her husband all respect.'

As if that were not enough, on the basis of the Adam and Eve stories (which Paul accepted as fact) Paul claimed that women were responsible for men's sinfulness.

In church, women were to cover their heads because their hair is their glory. They were to dress 'modestly and soberly' (like the Archbishop at the Coronation perhaps?) 'not decked out with gold or pearls or elaborate hair-styles.' 'A woman must be a learner listening quietly and with due submission, nor must woman domineer over man, she should be quiet.' In point of fact women were to be silent in church.

'Women should not address the meeting. They have no licence to speak. It is a shocking thing that a woman should address the congregation.' 'What I write has the Lord's authority.'

Clearly that shocking thing had already taken place. It must not be allowed to happen again. And until the middle of the twentieth century, through most of the Christian church (there were a few exceptions) it didn't. Paul's words were treated as if he really did have 'the Lord's authority' although no one ever tried to verify that claim.

If it were possible I would love to persuade my daughters to read all that Paul has to say about women and then I would introduce them to him. I would give them all a cup of tea and leave them with him for an hour or so. I suspect that it would be a very chastened St. Paul who emerged from that room.

Women have had to fight very hard to escape from ancient ideas of their place in the world. In many parts of the world those ancient ideas persist and even where they do not the battle continues.

Oddly enough it is often only where the church is seriously in decline that those ideas have been scrapped.

Apparently, on the subject of women, Paul's words were not the word of God. As a result we now have female priests and even bishops. A shortage of men offering for the priesthood has done wonders for the female cause within the church.

There is another area where Paul's thinking was very much of its time. But sadly, no one with any power questioned his attitude until the second half of the eighteenth century. The clergy never did. But to give credit where it is due, when people did at last see the wrongfulness of a pretty universal practice, it was largely evangelical Christians who sought to put things right. I'm writing, of course, about slavery. Paul never questioned slavery. His attitude was simply that masters should be good masters and slaves, good slaves. 'Obey your masters with fear and trembling, single-mindedly, serve whole-heartedly, cheerfully. The Lord will repay.'

The last letter of Paul in the New Testament is the brief letter to Philemon, and it is about Philemon's runaway slave, Onesimus.

Paul did not address the question of slavery. It was to be nearly another 1800 years before people began to do that. (It was not abolished in Mississippi until 1895.) And slavery is still with us. Instead, Paul said that Onesimus had wronged Philemon in running away. But we are not told why he had run away in the first place. If Philemon was such a good master, why run away? There is talk later of possible debts. Maybe it was a question of money and dishonesty. We cannot know.

Paul accepted the institution of slavery and therefore considered that Onesimus had wronged his master in running away. So he was sending him back. He asked (pleaded with) Philemon to welcome Onesimus back 'no longer as a slave, but as more than a slave – as a dear brother, both as a man and as a Christian. . . Welcome him as you would welcome me.'

So Christianity didn't alter the institution of slavery or the master/slave relationship as such. It only tried to make masters better masters and slaves better slaves, and then only if they were fellow Christians.

Paul's letter to Philemon was a lovely, warm, affectionate letter and it suggested that relationships between masters and slaves could be relationships of friendship. But Paul never questioned the institution. He didn't even talk about the possibility of masters setting their slaves free even though it was possible in the Roman world for slaves to achieve freedom.

There is just one more subject I want to touch on briefly in this chapter.

Paul told his fellow Christians to 'submit to the supreme authorities' because they are 'instituted by God. Consequently anyone who rebels against authority is resisting a divine institution and those who rebel have themselves to thank for the punishment they will receive.' 'The authorities. . . are God's agents working for your good.'

I don't think many Christians would agree with this. I certainly hope that they wouldn't. It was perhaps wise for a small minority community to keep its head down and to keep clear of politics. No sensible person wants to bring down the wrath of the powerful on himself. But how many Christians really believe that their political leaders were appointed by God.

I wonder whether Paul himself continued to believe that

the authorities were appointed by God when they condemned him to death.

This chapter has demonstrated very clearly how much a man of his own time Paul was. It has demonstrated how very wrong he could be on a variety of different subjects.

It is not for his opinions on these subjects that Paul is valued by Christians today. But if he could be so much a man of his own time and so often plainly wrong in his opinions, is it not at least possible that when it comes to subjects of central importance in religion and life he could be wrong too?

It is to those subjects that we must now turn our attention.

Chapter 3

The Law of God

I began this book with the claim that most of us want to live well. That doesn't mean that we spend much time thinking about it or trying to define what we mean by a good life. On the whole we just get on with things and, whatever we are doing, we do our best.

For Paul, with his ideas of God as our judge, living well was both essential and impossible. We are all of us wicked sinners, abject failures, ripe for the judgement of God and destined for rejection and exclusion from heaven.

As we have seen, Paul was a Jew. Originally known as Israelites, the Jews came from a number of tribes who were pretty unique in the ancient world in that they gave up belief in many local gods and spirits and focussed their belief in one supreme god. It took time but ultimately they came to believe that he was the *only* God. They were not yet ready to think the unthinkable, that there were no gods at all.

Believing in the one true God, they felt that their reward was that they became the people of God. As the people of God they were privileged to receive the law of God, the gold standard by which they were to live. They would be marked out from all other peoples by their belief in the one true God and their obedience to his law. Through their belief and their obedience they were saved from ignorance and error and became the chosen people.

And all of their belief related to this life. There was no belief in another life after death. For centuries their whole focus was on this life. Living it well, living it according to the will of God, meant obeying his law.

Because the first Christians were Jews the first Christian teachers were Jews. They assumed that Christians must obey God's law – that the law he had given to their people must apply to everyone. But, by now, their teaching had another dimension.

Some Jews, but by no means all of them, had developed a belief in a life after death. Thanks to their belief in the resurrection of Jesus, Christians adopted this belief and developed their ideas of the judgement of God with the separation of people (according to the teaching of Jesus) into sheep and goats – sheep destined for heaven and goats destined for hell.

It was natural for early Jewish Christians to assume that in order to go to heaven, they must obey the law of God. As Paul turned his attention entirely to people who were not Jews, he felt that he couldn't lay what he saw as the burden of the Law on their shoulders. He went on to offer another way. We shall turn to that in due course.

But he found himself walking something of a tightrope. He was angry when his fellow teachers demanded that non-Jews obey the Jewish law, but because that law was the law of God, he couldn't reject it entirely. After all, that would suggest that God was inconstant and fickle – that he didn't know his own mind.

And when you come to think about it, looking at religion

25

from the outside, it does look at though God may be fickle. First he chose the Jews to be his chosen people. Then he seems to have rejected then in favour of the Christians. And a few centuries later, another group came along with a different holy book, claiming that they had replaced both Jews and Christians. And so Moslems became the new people of God.

But I have allowed myself to become distracted. Let us return to Paul. I have already mentioned that he seems to have had little interest in the teaching of Jesus. He may not have known much about it. Nor does he seem to have had anything of the warmth of Jesus' affection for his fellow men and women. As we have seen, Paul seems to have believed that we are all fundamentally evil and in need of salvation from the judgement of God.

It is in his letter to the Roman Christians that he spelt out his beliefs about the way we can be saved. This is the first of his letters in the New Testament and it doesn't make for easy reading.

I can't stress bluntly enough the fact that Paul believed that we are all wicked sinners in need of salvation. He believed that we are destined to be judged by God either when we die, or at the final judgement at the end time. He believed that the end time was near and that it might even come during his lifetime.

Given global warming, people are beginning to think in terms of an end time again.

Without salvation, Paul believed that God's judgement upon us would be devastating. He doesn't paint the kind of lurid pictures of hell fire that his successors painted, but he would have approved them. Without salvation he believed that we were destined for hell. With salvation we are destined for heaven. Salvation would transform us from vile, wicked sinners to fine, godly people.

It will astonish Christians if I tell them that Paul actually spoke of three quite different paths to salvation. It would probably astonish Paul, too.

One of them appears in just one line and I shall leave it to the last. One of them is the Christian path. One of them is the pathway set before him as a Jew. That is the pathway I propose to look at first of all. It is the pathway of obedience to the law of God.

As we have seen, Paul was brought up within the Jewish religion. He believed that, a thousand or more years before Jesus, God had given his law to Moses. God had chosen the twelve tribes of Israel to be his own people. If they kept his law they would always have that privileged status.

'They were made God's sons,' [forget the daughters!]
'Theirs is the splendour of the divine presence,
  theirs the covenants,
  the law, the temple worship,
  and God's promises.'

So the Jews were a privileged people who had been given special knowledge of God through the law given to Moses. That law set them above their fellow men and enabled them to become the world's teachers 'to guide the blind, to enlighten the benighted, to train the stupid, and to teach the immature.' Paul really didn't have a very high opinion of most of us.

The rite of circumcision marked Jews out from their fellows. Similarly, the rite of baptism marked Christians out from their fellows. But it was no good relying on such rites to give a special, personal relationship with God. The law of God was useless unless people kept it.

Although Paul was writing to his fellow Jews, the principle is clear. If anyone has found a religion or philosophy which shows the right way to live, it is meaningless unless they actually live by it. Similarly, those who claim to be our moral teachers must live by their teaching.

So what were non-Jewish Christians to make of the law? Many early Christian teachers (Jewish Christians) said that they must obey it. As a sign of that obedience, they must begin by being circumcised. Oddly enough, when I was a child, many Christian parents still had their baby boys circumcised because it was 'in the Bible'.

Paul disagreed with such teachers and if Paul disagreed with you, you soon knew it. He was never one to mince his words. Yet he had to be careful. He tried to walk a tightrope, claiming that Christians did not have to obey the *ritual* requirements of the Law. But he could hardly deny that obedience to the fundamentals of the Law – the Law of God remember – would lead to godly lives.

The trouble with law is that it can so easily become a kind of straight-jacket, all-embracing and nit-picking, attempting to cover every tiny eventuality. And there are times when even apparently good laws need to be set on one side. Victor Hugo's book *Les Miserables*, best known now through the musical, demonstrates that sometimes we should set on one side the law 'thou shalt not steal'.

If Paul had been around in time to hear Jesus teaching he would have heard him say that 'the (Sabbath) law was made for man, not man for the Sabbath.' And he would have heard Jesus summarise the law very simply, telling people to love God and to love their neighbour as themselves. Jesus considered that was all people needed to know about the law, and that if they followed that simple instruction they wouldn't go far wrong.

If we wish to obey the law of God without being scholars or knowledgeable clergy, all we have to do is to love God and love our neighbour. And if we don't happen to believe in God then we can reduce this still further and content ourselves with loving our neighbour.

At which point some wag in the classroom will mutter, 'and what about my neighbour's wife?'

And that will lead us to ask what Jesus meant by the word 'love' in this context. Clearly not sexual love: love in this context simply means doing our best for. It includes such things as friendliness, kindness, thoughtfulness and so on. To ordinary people that is all so obvious that I don't need to go on about it. If we obey the Law as Jesus simplified it we shall live good lives. It is as simple as that.

But Paul never managed to achieve that kind of simplicity. However, he claimed that Christians were excused from keeping the ritual requirements of the Law. In one practical area of life, that was very important. Much of the meat that you could buy at the butcher's had been offered in pagan shrines to the gods.

The meat from such sacrifices was not wasted. The gods fed on the smell of roasting meat. The best of the cuts went to the priests and the rest went to the butchers. So, if you were a Christian what were you to do? Could you buy and eat meat from pagan sacrifices? If you couldn't, you were left with very little choice. Paul said that they were free to eat it, but that they should always consider the thoughts and feelings of those who were more sensitive or squeamish than they were.

Following on from Paul, few Christians have bothered to

follow the minute details of Jewish Law. But they have often tried to follow the most famous summary of all – oddly enough, not the summary of Jesus which I mentioned just now, but the summary known as 'the Ten Commandments' which you used to find on many a church or chapel wall.

Christians clearly felt that if you obeyed those ten (mostly negative) commandments, you wouldn't go far wrong, and at the judgement day you would be found acceptable to God.

In these basic ways then, the Church has always believed that salvation is possible for those who obey the Law of God. That is the earliest path of salvation and offers a way in which we can guarantee that we shall live good lives.

I'm not sure that Paul would agree with that last paragraph. Nor would the evangelical wing of the church. Their view of the vileness of most of us means that they believe that something much more desperate was needed if we were to be saved from the judgement of God.

Some early Christian teachers were not content that pagan converts should simply obey Jesus' summary of the Law. They insisted that it must be followed in detail. New Christians must be circumcised. Paul was so angry that he fell off his tightrope. In his letter to the Galatians he wrote:

'No man is ever justified by doing what the law demands, but only through faith in Jesus Christ. My present bodily life is lived by faith in the Son of God who loved me and sacrificed himself for me.'

Paul was so angry that he wrote, 'If anyone should preach a gospel at variance with the gospel we preached to you, he shall be held outcast.'

I think it was the Roman Governor Pliny who said sarcastically, 'See how these Christians love one another.'

Paul grew angry with another set of Christians who listened to him setting the Law on one side and promptly assumed that he meant that they could live as they liked. Because they were justified by the sacrifice of Jesus, they were free to live in whatever way they wished. Paul wasn't happy with that either. 'You were called to be free men. . . only do not turn your freedom into licence for your lower nature.'

So, if something more than the law of God was needed, what was it? We must turn to his picture of salvation, the picture that evangelical Christians have always followed.

Chapter 4

Salvation: The Evangelical Christian View

Paul believed in God as the almighty creator of the world and everything in it. He believed that human beings are subject to the judgement of God. Based on that judgement they are destined, after this life, for heaven or hell.

Now that he was a Christian, Paul believed that there is only one way to be saved from the judgement of God and to avoid hell. He set out to show how we can become acceptable to God and how we can receive his gift of life after death in everlasting bliss.

He began with the claim that we are all sinners in need of salvation. He went on to claim that we can all be saved through faith in Jesus and his death on the cross. At its simplest, the idea is that Jesus offered himself to God as a perfect human sacrifice on behalf of all of us and God accepted that sacrifice. Through faith in that sacrifice, we can be saved.

Those who believe neither in God nor in life after death may wonder what on earth any of this has to do with them.

In one sense: nothing.

But gods of one kind or another have played a very significant part in human life for a very long time. Perhaps

32

those of us who are irreligious can learn from an understanding of the things that make religious people tick.

Paul claimed that 'all that may be known of God by men' has 'been visible since the world began.'

If that is true, one wonders why there has ever been any need for religion of any kind. We can see and know God 'in the things he has made' without ever needing teachers, and we can respond to what we learn in our own ways.

Perhaps that might have been possible. The trouble is we are such vile creatures!

And at once we can begin to see the flaws in the Christian teaching about salvation.

How bad do you have to be in order to need salvation? How many of us really are 'wicked sinners'? Oh yes, I know that it is true that many of us, given the right circumstances, are capable of being pretty vile. But is that our norm? If evangelists came down from the pulpit and stopped preaching for a while and actually mixed with people or worked amongst them, they would sing a different song. For most people are pretty decent on the whole.

But the Christian doctrine of salvation requires that we need to be bad enough to need saving. How bad?

According to Paul we are all really bad.

Paul's hostility towards the human race is quite incredible. We are all godless and wicked, vile and degraded given up to shameless, unnatural passions. In particular he had it in for men and women who 'have given up natural intercourse for unnatural.' I'm not sure whether it was just those, or whether it was all of us, who Paul described with such brilliant hostility. We are 'one mass of envy, murder, rivalry, treachery and malevolence.'

33

The description went on and on. How Paul must have hated and despised his fellow men.

No wonder they needed his gospel.

But are we really as bad as all that? I live in a small village on the edge of a small town. I doubt if there is a single person in our village who fits Paul's description. And what about the town? According to the local newspaper there is occasional anti-social behaviour: a few drunks fighting; some thieving; a few kids damaging other people's cars; a few people found with drugs; even an occasional – very occasional – incident of arson.

I'm over ninety years old and I've met an awful lot of people in my life-time. I haven't liked everyone I've met but some of them have probably disliked me too. But there isn't one of the people I have met who I would describe in the kind of language Paul used. Not one.

Most of them have been decent and kind, living decent lives – not saints, but genuine, warm friendly people.

Paul and his fellow evangelists can't accept that. If people need salvation, they must be evil. And Paul promised wicked people 'the fury of retribution, grinding misery for every human being who is an evil doer.'

There then is the first flaw in the Christian doctrine of salvation. It paints a picture of human beings which is false. It is anxious to show that every one of us needs salvation and it never asks 'How bad do we need to be before we need salvation?' I shall return to that question later. For now, let's return to Paul.

In contrast with our awfulness Paul painted a picture of a 'God full of kindness, patience and tolerance.' This God will give 'glory, honour and immortality – eternal life.'

But who will God give these gifts to? Who will he save?

And it is here that the second flaw in the Christian doctrine of salvation is revealed. If the first flaw was an insult to most human beings the second demeans the Christian God.

It was Jesus who taught people to pray 'Our Father...'. And it was Jesus who taught the parable of the prodigal son, where a young man has squandered his inheritance and ended up poverty stricken before going home and being welcomed by his father.

After the most serious crisis of my own life, brought on by myself, I returned home to my parents. Without any questions, they took me back in and gave me their love.

Paul himself spoke of God as 'full of kindness, patience and tolerance'. Won't such a God, kind, patient, tolerant, parental, welcome most of us with open arms even if we have not been quite the wonderful people he hoped we might be?

Apparently not.

We have to be saved 'All alike have sinned and are deprived of the divine splendour.' We are back with all those evangelical preachers who love to tell us what wicked sinners we are, all outside the pale. All of us without exception need to be saved and according to them, there is only one path of salvation. Only one.

We are saved by faith in Jesus and his sacrifice on the cross. That is the only way.

That means, of course, that there are multitudes of people who can never be saved. This God is an unfair God.

Think of all those generations of human beings spreading slowly throughout the world who lived before Jesus. They never heard the gospel. Think of all those people all over the world since the time of Jesus who have never heard the gospel. Think of all the people in our own time who have never heard it and of all those people in the future who will never hear it.

This wonderful gospel of salvation has never been offered to more than a tiny minority of the human race. If every single one of us needs to be saved and if there is only one path of salvation, either that path needs to be offered to everyone or God is unjust.

Think last of those few people who did actually hear the teaching of Jesus and put their faith in him *and died before him*. There wouldn't be many of them. Was it enough that they put their faith in him as a result of his teaching? After all, they knew nothing of his sacrifice. And if it was enough why is it not enough for the rest of us? Why did Jesus have to die?

There is a somewhat unconvincing 'Get out of Jail' card which Christians played although I have never heard it used. They claim that after his death he went and preached to all dead souls, thus giving them the opportunity to put their faith in him. Do they also believe that he has met every single soul since, after each individual death (or all those souls who died on the first day of the battle of the Somme) and given them their chance?

If he didn't, then God is unjust – and surely, if you believe in God, that is unthinkable.

Which brings us finally to the question of the sacrifice of Jesus on the Cross.

For most of the ministry of Jesus he seems to have been content to spend his time teaching and healing. There was no plan, no feeling that he was heading towards anything in particular, no ultimate goal in sight. But then, during the final week, he went head on with the religious and political authorities, but still without seeming to know what he was trying to achieve. If the gospels can be believed, the only thing he seemed sure of was that his challenge to authority would lead to his death.

He was right. But what did he believe that death would achieve? Did he really see himself as a sacrifice offered to God on behalf of the rest of us? If so, it seems very odd. After all, he thought of God as his Father and of himself as God's son – perhaps even Son with a capital letter.

Round about two thousand years before Jesus lived, one of the great forefathers of the Jewish nation came to feel that he must offer his son Isaac as a sacrifice to God. This son had only been born after a long period of trying, and now he had to be given back to God. His father, Abraham, must have been heart-broken but such was his devotion to God that he set out to make the sacrifice. The story is told with great poignancy in the book of Genesis.

In the event God showed Abraham, not only that he did not want the sacrifice of Isaac, but that he did not want any human sacrifice. Jesus would have known that story. So how could he have possibly thought that God required him to sacrifice himself? What on earth does that say about his teaching that God is 'our Father'?

In a little while I also want to consider the fact that Christians believe that Jesus was not only a perfect man, he is also God, one of the three persons of the Trinity. That makes this idea of sacrifice even more incredible. How does God sacrifice himself to himself? The whole conception is ridiculous.

Setting all that on one side we can ask similar questions about the beliefs and teaching of Paul and of Christian teachers ever since. They have always claimed that Jesus is the means of achieving forgiveness and release from our sins and that he managed this by his sacrificial death for us.

Paul and his fellows tell us that God will overlook our sins and justify anyone who puts his faith in Jesus and his sacrifice. They tell us that this sacrifice was necessary in order to win our salvation. God required the sacrifice of a perfect human being on the cross.

The same question arises again:

Isn't God supposed to be our heavenly parent; just, good and loving?' Isn't it a complete denial of all his/her goodness to suggest that s/he required such a sacrifice. Is s/he really that horrible? How many human parents would behave in such a way? Are we nobler than God?

And here is another question – one which many people have asked down through the centuries and which many Christian thinkers have tried in vain to answer:

HOW does the death of one man save the soul of another?

Lots of thinkers have tried to answer that question. Each of them has come up with answers but none of them really satisfies. When I was a student, a Methodist scholar called Vincent Taylor examined those answers, found them wanting and tried to come up with answers of his own. I don't think he was fully satisfied even then.

The simple truth is that we can sometimes save someone else – say from drowning or from a house fire. But there is no way that the sacrifice of one man, even if he was perfect (and we have seen that even Jesus was not perfect), could achieve all that this death was supposed to achieve. And it still leaves unanswerable questions about the kind of God to whom such a sacrifice would be acceptable.

Paul's doctrine of salvation – the Christian doctrine of

salvation – is flawed over and over again. It raises serious questions about the nature of the Christian God.

The Christian idea of salvation through the sacrifice of Jesus only succeeds in its appeal if you do not think about it too carefully. At its simplest the Christian claim is that on the Cross Jesus offered himself as a perfect sacrifice on behalf of all of us. Those who place their faith in him are saved from the awful judgement of God.

There is no doubt that there are some people whose lives have been transformed by their belief in this sacrifice. It is wonderful that that is the case.

It doesn't alter the fact that people's lives can he transformed in a variety of different ways; through meeting and marrying the right husband or wife; through coming into contact with the right counsellor or psychiatrist; just through an ordinary or extraordinary personal awakening. Religion is not necessarily a part of this at all.

And, as I mentioned in passing, Christian ideas of the sacrifice are further complicated by their ideas of the nature of God himself.

Christians believe that, in himself, Jesus combines two natures. To them, Jesus was a perfect man and is also God, the second person of the Trinity. It is a complex and mind-boggling belief. It was once my own belief.

But I now believe that a close examination of the Gospels demonstrates that although Jesus was a fine man, he certainly wasn't perfect. And what of the belief that Jesus is God?

Paul expressed that belief – especially in his letter to the Colossians, 1, 15-20: 'In him the complete being of God came to dwell.' The belief was also expressed very beautifully in John's first chapter when he came to write his

Gospel. It is an incredible concept and, for many thinking Christians, it is the summit of their belief.

But it was a belief which divided Christians from the start. Some of them didn't believe that Jesus was God. Some of them felt that he wasn't really a man like the rest of us. Arguments broke out, divisions, persecution and death followed. The Church was divided from the start and over the centuries there has been a great deal of cruelty and slaughter: one set of believers against another.

But if we return to the Christian idea of salvation we find that the orthodox idea of Jesus as both a man and God makes a nonsense of the whole idea. Can God sacrifice himself to himself?

And since, by definition, God cannot die, we have to ask ourselves what actually happened on the Cross. Jesus cried out, 'My God, my God, why hast thou forsaken me?' Was that the moment when the divine Jesus left the human Jesus to die alone? Did the divine element in the nature of Jesus leave the human body at some point to its natural end?

Of course, Christians also believe in the resurrection of Jesus from death. In fact, Paul went so far as to say that without the resurrection, Christian faith was meaningless.

I don't believe in the resurrection, but if I did, what are we to say of the divine element in the nature of Jesus. Did it leave the body before death and then return at the resurrection, taking the manhood of Jesus into the nature of God?

These ideas are so obscure and so completely unanswerable that they play havoc with the simple Christian idea of salvation.

Setting all of this on one side, we must go on to ask 'what is salvation anyway?'

Chapter 5

What is Salvation?

We have already seen just what Paul thought of his neighbours. We are all of us slaves of sin. Although evangelical preachers love to dwell on our wickedness, there is no need for me to waste more time on the subject. The Christian claim is that, through the death of Jesus on the cross we can be saved from our sins.

There is no doubt that there are some people whose lives are transformed through faith in that 'sacrifice'. There is also no doubt that there are some people whose lives are transformed without any intervention from religion at all. Such transformations have much more to do with our psychology than they do with religion.

But regardless of all that, what is this salvation supposed to achieve? Won't it achieve it for ALL Christians? If they are saved from sin does this mean that they will become sinless?

That was something which exercised the early Methodists. Were Christians supposed to be perfect? It really worried them. After all, who on earth can claim to be perfect? The early Methodists came up with a compromise. Christians could and should become perfect in love.

But if you read Paul's letters to the Corinthians it is very plain that they often didn't.

The Corinthian Christians did not, it seems, have the Spirit of God. They were still on the natural plane. There was jealousy and strife among them. There was sexual immorality. They were 'so-called Christians who were grasping, drunkards, swindlers.'

While Paul urged the Corinthians to 'root out evil doers from their community,' the rest of us can't help wondering how they were there in the first place. This Corinthian Christian church sounds to have been no better, and perhaps a good deal worse, than many another group or club.

Paul went on to speak of the need to grow, aided by their teachers. 'We are God's fellow workers and you are God's garden.'

He wrote sarcastically, comparing the self-regarding qualities and strengths of the Corinthians and the failings and weaknesses of their teachers, including himself. He pleaded with them to follow his example and he also threatened them:

'Am I to come to you with a rod in my hand or in love and in a gentle spirit?'

The Corinthian Christians really do seem to have been a contentious crowd. Like present day Americans and increasingly ourselves, they took their disputes to the law-courts instead of sorting them out themselves. Paul was almost despairing and wrote 'to shame' them. Here were Christians who, by definition, were going to judge the rest of the sinful world, and they couldn't even sort out their own trivial disputes. 'You fall below your standard in going to law with one another.' 'Surely you know that the unjust will never come into possession of the kingdom of God.'

And then Paul really went to town, listing some of those who will never come into possession of the kingdom of God: 'no fornicator or idolater, none who are guilty of adultery or of homosexual perversion, no thieves or grabbers, or drunkards or slanderers or swindlers.'

When you read that, it is no wonder that the Church gets into such chaos when it tries to sort out its attitude to the LBGT community.

Paul claimed that some of the Corinthians 'had been people of the kinds he has just damned so fiercely but they had been through the purifying waters' yet it doesn't seem to have made all that much difference to them. Unfortunately they had misunderstood the meaning of salvation. Having been justified, saved from sin, and brought into the family of God, they now felt that salvation gave them complete freedom to live as they wished – including apparently the freedom to express their lusts and to use prostitutes.

Paul reminded them that their bodies were 'limbs and organs of Christ. . . He who links himself with Christ is one with him spiritually.' 'Your body is a shrine to the indwelling Holy Spirit. . . you do not belong to yourselves, you were bought at a price (the price of the sacrifice of Jesus). Then honour God in your body.'

It seems amazing that Paul should have to write such things if the Christian religion is all that it is cracked up to be. Christians are no different from the rest of us – certainly no better. These Corinthian Christians were a good deal worse.

In another of his letters (Ephesians) Paul showed that he could be full of pride, gratitude and affection for the quality of his fellow Christians, but that certainly wasn't the case with the Corinthians. He was scathing.

My own experience within the church was that most people and most clergy were thoroughly decent, good, honourable and likeable, but that wasn't always true. Since leaving the church and dealing as closely with people as I did when I was a minister I have felt exactly the same way about people generally – most of them are thoroughly decent, good, honourable and likeable.

If Christian salvation theology was true, you would expect there to be a marked difference in quality between Christians and the rest of us. There isn't. Christians often claim that there is, but they are wrong. There isn't.

We have seen that salvation claimed to free people from ritual demands and from slavery to sin. Finally it saves us from the judgement of God.

Paul and many of his fellows believed that they were living in the end time. Possibly during their own lifetimes Jesus would return in great power and glory and bring in the final judgement of God when the 'sheep' would be separated from the 'goats'. The sheep would move on to enjoy everlasting bliss and the goats would be consigned to the everlasting fires of hell.

It didn't happen then and it hasn't happened since, although with global warming people are beginning to wonder whether our time as a species is nearly up.

In my childhood there were still plenty of people within the Roman Catholic church and on the more extreme edges of the Protestant churches who loved to try to terrify people into faith with their stories of hell-fire. Look at any ancient murals and you will see that it is far easier to paint vivid pictures of hell than it is to depict the wonders of heaven. There are all those devils poking souls with their pronged forks and submerging them in the bubbling cauldrons of human soup, boiling away, on and on for ever in waters heated by the everlasting flames of hell.

Salvation releases us from the judgement of God.

I suspect that there are not many people who find this of any significance nowadays. It has always made me wonder what sort of a God Paul, and even Jesus, believed in. Jesus may have told us to pray to our 'Father' but the God of judgement doesn't seem much like a Father to me.

On so many levels and in so many ways the whole business of salvation seems so flawed. It depends upon people being a great deal worse than they are and it paints pictures which are utterly unconvincing; and finally, it makes claims that just don't stand up to scrutiny.

But none of this alters the fact that faith in Jesus can lead to the transformation of a bad life. If it does, that is a truly wonderful thing and I wouldn't want anything I say to undermine its value.

But even where that happens, salvation is only a beginning; the turning of a new page or the opening of a new chapter – a January 1st moment.

The intention of salvation is that it should lead to good, godly lives. Salvation is no more than the key which unlocks the door. Good lives have to be lived day by day with absolute consistency from the day of salvation onwards.

I do not share Paul's jaundiced view of people. While there are bad eggs, I do not believe that most people need salvation in the first place. Some do but most do not. So, while the road to a good life may begin in some form of salvation experience, for most people it is the road they have always walked. Goodness, decency, kindness, honesty, integrity, thoughtfulness, courage, hard work and love mark most people from the beginning of their lives right through to the end.

Just as we have no need for laws to tell us how to live, so we have no need of a great salvation experience to turn us from evil to good.

For Christians, the whole business of salvation is summed up in their central act of worship. Perhaps it will be worthwhile having a look at that central rite.

Chapter 6

The Lord's Supper
1 Corinthians Chapters 10 16-17 & 11 16-34.

The last supper Jesus shared with his closest disciples is remembered by various names today: the Lord's Supper, the Holy Communion, or the Eucharist. In Paul's time that remembrance had not become completely divorced from ordinary Christian social eating and drinking or turned into a central rite of Christian worship.

At Corinth, and no doubt elsewhere, it is clear that there was an ideal of people bringing food for a congregation to share, the better off bringing more and the poor benefitting from their generosity: except that in Corinth, it didn't work like that.

In this dysfunctional church people fell into sharply divided groups. The better off ate their own food and drank their own wine and left the poor to go hungry and thirsty.

Paul was disgusted. That was a total denial of what the Lord's Supper was all about. 'Are you so contemptuous of the church of God that you shame its poorer members?'

So Paul reminded them of what happened when Jesus broke bread and shared it with his closest followers and when they shared the wine. He reminded them, both of the

47

facts and of the meaning of what became the Christian sacrament.

First, the facts:

Jesus took the cup and said, 'This cup is the new Covenant' (binding agreement between God and Christians) 'sealed by my blood.' And Jesus took 'bread, broke it, and said, 'This is my body, which is for you.' Christians were to eat and drink in memory of Jesus.

But this was intended to be much more than just a memorial meal. It was intended as an act of communion both with Jesus and with one another. 'When we bless the cup of blessing, is it not a means of sharing in the blood of Christ? When we break the bread, is it not a means of sharing in the body of Christ? Because there is one loaf, we, many as we are, are one body.'

It followed that anyone who ate or drank unworthily desecrated the body and blood of Jesus. 'Therefore my brothers (as so often with Paul, the sisters do not seem to have been considered) – therefore my brothers, when you meet for a meal, wait for one another.' 'If you are hungry, eat at home.'

It is sad that Paul's teaching on the Lord's Supper had to end on such a banal note, but the Corinthian Christians were so clearly self-centred that they needed such instructions.

In a sense, this passage in Paul is a prelude to the whole sorry saga of this central rite of Christianity.

At its best, it is a deeply moving sacrament, and for believers it can be the heart of their worship. It can be a communal, shared, yet intimately personal time when the worshippers feel at one with their God and with one another.

But it clearly wasn't that at Corinth. Sadly for believers,

over the centuries this rite has become one of the most significant signs of the divisions between them. Christians of one brand of the church are not allowed to share in this rite with Christians of another brand. Catholics cannot partake with Protestants and some Protestants cannot partake with others.

For those who care about such things it is deeply saddening. The churches are fatally flawed. Just at the point where they should be most at one, heart bound to heart, life to life, they are most completely divided. This is a complete rejection of the prayer of their Lord 'that they may be one as I and the Father are one.'

But as Paul has revealed all too clearly in this letter to the Corinthians, in spite of all their talk of salvation, and the difference it makes to people, Christians are no different and no better than the rest of us. Sometimes, as in Corinth, their quarrelsome, squabbling behaviour suggests that they may be even worse.

c

Chapter 7

The Value of Salvation

Christians will feel that I have not done justice to their conception of salvation.

First of all, the very idea of someone sacrificing himself for others is much more appealing than I have suggested.

Secondly, according to Paul, through his sacrifice, Jesus became the sole mediator between us and God. It is only through him that we can have a relationship with God. No one else can bring us to God's footstool.

Third, his sacrifice brings us the gifts of the Holy Spirit, which we in turn are expected to use on behalf of our fellows.

Let us have a look at each of those statements in turn.

The idea of someone sacrificing himself for someone else is immensely impressive: a parent for a child, a friend for a friend, even someone for a stranger. We are moved by such sacrifices. Even if we think that Jesus was misguided we can still admire him for his willingness to die on behalf of the rest of us.

Paul claimed that through his sacrifice Jesus became the sole mediator between us and God, that no one else can enable us to have a relationship with God. That is an immense claim. In his mind, and in the mind of Christians generally, there is no other teacher to compare with Jesus. No one else comes near him.

I can understand Christians believing that, but they will only continue to believe it if they never examine the teaching of others.

I had felt that I wanted simply to underline some of the 'benefits' of salvation without comment or criticism. But I find that I cannot let these things rest. Some of my questions and criticisms of the first value of salvation have already been expressed. But this second one has not been considered.

Those of us who do not believe in any kind of God will find Paul's idea of a mediator between us and God meaningless. And if we did believe in some sort of supreme being, God over all, the question arises: would he have the slightest interest in little me and would I have any real wish to be in contact with him?

Speaking for myself – and 1 cannot speak for anyone else – the answer is 'no'.

Their God is too remote, too important. Just as I haven't the remotest interest in being introduced to either the king and queen or the prime minister, and just as they would not have the remotest interest in being introduced to me, so I have no desire to be introduced to a God who will interfere with my life and aim to dominate it.

The third Christian claim is that salvation brings us the gifts of the Holy Spirit, gifts which are to be used for the benefit of the whole community.

This is the kind of claim that can never be substantiated in any meaningful way. But it is also a claim which cannot be denied in any meaningful way either.

Paul claimed that Christians are imbued with the spirit of God. As a result they know God, they know his gifts and they possess 'the mind of Christ.'

There is no arguing with claims like these. There is no room for discussion or debate. Either you believe them or you do not.

What they ought to mean is that Christians become pretty special people. Some of them do. But as a non-Christian I would want to add that there are plenty of very special people who are not Christians and who have no religious beliefs at all.

The second gift of salvation is membership of the church – the family of God. We have already seen that, even in Paul's day, the church was not necessarily a very happy or united family. Paul was proud of the church in Ephesus and disgusted by the church in Corinth.

I've known plenty of churches that weren't up to much and I suspect that many of them have closed in the time since I knew them.

But the church at its best can be a wonderful congregation of like-minded people – open, welcoming, full of friendship – a real kind of extended family. In such churches, worship becomes a pleasure and an inspiration and the wider life of the church is full of the pleasures of real friendship and companionship. Such churches are immensely valuable to all who belong to them and they often reach out in valuable ways to many who do not belong to them. The church at its best is a very valuable part of its local community and it can reach out very far indeed.

I don't want to undermine what I have just said except to add that for many of us, there are other organisations which provide a very similar kind of warmth and sense of family and service.

The gift of the Spirit of God and the place within the Christian family should lead to the third gift of salvation: lives of real quality. In a number of his letters Paul urged his readers to live such lives and produced lists of the qualities he would expect to find in Christian lives. Those lists are wholly admirable. Because they are lists of the kind of virtues we would expect to find in any decent life, Christian or not, I propose to leave them until almost the very end of this book. It is enough here to notice that Paul expected salvation to lead to lives of the very first quality. One of the values of the Christian church is that it does strive to persuade people to live good lives and it does try to help them to do so.

The final gift of salvation is resurrection from death to everlasting paradise. Paul expressed his belief in resurrection in fair detail in Romans 15 and 16. I want to look at that in the next chapter.

But what of paradise?

As already mentioned, it has always seemed curious to me that it is so much easier, whether with words or in pictures, to paint vivid pictures of hell-fire than it is to depict the perfect bliss of heaven. Noel Coward wrote a marvellously amusing poem about his inability to believe in the kind of heaven that is on offer. It began:

> I gaze at the immensities of blue
> And say to myself, 'It can't be true
> That somewhere in that abstract sphere
> Are all the people who were here'.

For most people, it seems to me, the one real reason they want to believe in heaven is that they hope for reunion with all those people they love who have died. But the Christian gospel doesn't offer that kind of reunion. Apparently it is enough to be in the presence of God and his angels.

I don't think there are many people nowadays who are excited by such a belief. For many of us the whole idea of heaven is meaningless. For me, it is enough to have lived and to have made the most of the one life I have. As with everything else in the world of nature, death simply marks the end of my personal little journey. There is nothing beyond nor do I wish there to be.

But I have been exceptionally lucky. I have had a pretty healthy life and a pretty long life, free from all the awfulness of long term illness or the horrors of war or poverty, hunger and worse. Perhaps if I had endured any of those things, I would try to take comfort in the thought of a possible hereafter life in some kind of heaven. Who knows?

Chapter 8

Resurrection
Romans Chapters 15 & 16.

This chapter is a complex one based on the claim that Jesus rose from the dead. For Christians it is triumphant and thrilling. But it depends almost entirely on that fundamental claim that Jesus rose from the dead.

That claim is not one that can be discussed rationally. Either you believe it and find a great deal in this chapter to thrill you, or you don't, in which case most of what Paul had to say is meaningless.

Paul regarded the resurrection as a 'fact' validated by the appearances of Jesus which were later to be recorded in the gospels and also validated by his own conversion experience. But to him, the resurrection was not just one fact among many. It was the foundation claim on which the whole Christian faith was built. 'If Christ was not raised, then our gospel is null and void, and so is your faith.'

In my book on Jesus for a secular age I have shown from Matthew's Gospel that there is every reason to believe that there was no resurrection. Many people would say that we don't actually need reasons. They would simply say, 'Resurrection doesn't happen. Therefore Jesus didn't rise.'

As a boy, brought up within the Christian faith, it never occurred to me to doubt that Jesus rose from death to life again. And when Matthew wrote of an earthquake at the time of Jesus' death the significance of that fact was lost on me. If I thought about it at all, I felt that he mentioned it just to add dramatic effect to the whole story, especially with the damage suffered by the Temple in Jerusalem.

It never dawned on me that that earthquake explained everything – how the stone was rolled away from Jesus' tomb and the loss of his body from his tomb through the cracks in the earth. Some of his down to earth female disciples recognised the truth, while other, more gullible disciples came up with their stories of resurrection.

If you read the stories surrounding the birth of Jesus and recognise that they are just stories, many of them quite attractive stories, you will not be surprised to find that his death became the subject of more stories – just stories. And many of those are quite attractive too.

Paul believed that without the resurrection there was nothing left. 'If it is for this life only that Christ has given us hope, we of all men are most to be pitied.'

To me that is excessively gloomy. There are elements in the teaching of Jesus which are of permanent worth. And my own response to Paul would be, 'If we can't find enough in this life to make it worth living to the full, then we are most to be pitied.'

But Paul was certain that the resurrection had taken place and that those who believed in Jesus would be raised too. 'But you may ask how are the dead raised? In what kind of body?'

Paul said that that was a senseless question, but he went on to try to answer it all the same. He spoke of our animal

56

bodies in this life and of our spiritual bodies in the next. 'Flesh and blood can never possess the kingdom of God.'

Finally Paul spoke of the end time when those who were still alive would not die but would be 'changed in a flash, in the twinkling of an eye' and 'this perishable' would 'be clothed in the imperishable. Then 'death would be swallowed up in victory.'

It is stirring stuff.

But it does all depend on belief in resurrection. Given what Paul had to say about physical bodies and spiritual bodies, it is curious that so many of the resurrection stories focus on the physical body of Jesus.

Paul's chapter ends with a resounding affirmation of his faith, much loved and much quoted by Christians:

'Death is swallowed up, victory is won!'

'Oh death, where is your victory? Oh death, where is your sting?'

The idea of resurrection was comparatively new in Paul's time. For centuries the Jews had managed perfectly well without such ideas. But then the Hasidim (forerunners of the Pharisees) came up with this new idea and it caught on. Perhaps death was not the end after all.

By the time of Jesus, the Jews were divided. The Sadducees did not believe in resurrection, the Pharisees did. No doubt ordinary people were divided. They still are, although in my experience, very few people have anything approaching Christian ideas. And many of us are quite content with the acceptance that we are simply a part of the animal kingdom. When our lives are over they are over – full stop.

In actual fact, the sting of death is not death itself. The sting of death is felt, not by the person who dies, but by those who are left. The sting of death is the sting of separation from those we love, and it is universal. It has nothing to do with religion or faith in life after death, or in any of the things Paul has been talking about in this chapter. It has to do with ordinary human love and loss. Some people will find it comforting to believe in the possibility of reunion in a future life after death. But oddly enough the idea of reunion never appeared either in the teaching of Jesus or in the teaching of Paul. The nearest Jesus came to talking about it was about as discouraging as possible. He said something along the lines of 'there is no marrying or giving in marriage in heaven.' Both Jesus and Paul assumed that we would no longer need each other in heaven – only God.

For me, there is no resurrection. The sting of the loss through death is real, but, like every other human experience, it can be woven into the rich tapestry of our lives in such a way that we can go on living – really living – after the death of those closest to us.

Chapter 9

God

Perhaps, after all this talk of salvation, it is time to look at the God who requires our salvation. Forgive me for using the masculine forms when I speak of God. I do know that belief in God is belief in a Spirit but I shall find it easier to speak of him in the traditional way.

Three religions claim to believe in one God. To Jews, Christians and Moslems there is only one God. He is supreme and alone. As we shall see, Christians complicate their picture of the one God, but for now we'll content ourselves with this concept of God as the one and only deity.

He is thought of as almighty, unchangeable, universal, omnipresent and all-knowing. I'm sure I've missed some of his attributes but these will do for the time being.

God is seen as the creator of everything. Believers are no longer tied to any particular ideas on how creation took place. Most people no longer believe the Genesis account of God creating over a period of six 'days' and then resting. But religious people do still look upon God as our creator.

And clearly the Creator has become pretty fed up with one of his creations. Humans have not turned out as he wished. In our own time, as we see how many species are becoming extinct through our behaviour and as we confront or fail to confront the realities of global warming we can well understand that God would not be very pleased with us.

Since, in addition to being our creator, he is also Almighty, you would think that he both could and would do something about us. Does he not care enough for the rest of his creation to protect other creatures from our behaviour? Is he not concerned enough about global warming to do something about it?

Apparently not. Although he is Almighty, he never uses his power either for our benefit or for the benefit of other creatures being driven to extinction.

As I write, Russians are invading Ukraine and Ukrainians are doing their best to resist. Meanwhile, a little while ago Hamas gave the Israelis a nasty shock and now the Israelis are turning Gaza into a heap of rubble and a cemetery. And God: The almighty Lord God? God of the Orthodox Church in Russia and in Ukraine; God of both Hamas and Israel; he does nothing.

In the midst of all this mayhem a little tiny voice is telling us to obey his law and/or to put our faith in Jesus and his sacrifice, or to follow the teachings of the Koran. But the Almighty Lord God leaves it all up to us no matter what we are doing to one another or to the rest of his creation.

Another of God's attributes as Spirit, is the ability to be everywhere at the same time and to be all-seeing. In my youth, these attributes were often used to try to scare children into what their adults thought of as good behaviour – things like subservience, obedience, and so on. As a result, some children were scared stiff of him and others of us learned to take no notice of what adults had to say about him.

He is also Omniscient – he knows everything. In Paul's letter to the Romans there is a glorious passage in chapter eight verses 13-39. But in the two verses before that passage he reminded his readers that God is all-knowing.

Think about that for a moment. He knows which of us will remain Jewish by their faith, which of us will become Christians and which of us will become Moslems. He also knows that in the two most populous parts of the world, India and China, almost nobody will become any of these three.

Surely that is a significant fact. The God we have been talking about is a middle Eastern/North African God brought by one imperial power to Europe and by other imperial powers to the rest of the world.

But it has made little headway in India. There, Hinduism, with its multitudes of gods and spirits has led, both in itself and in some of its offshoots – notably atheistic Buddhism – to a spiritual philosophy that many feel goes beyond anything on offer in the monotheistic religions. Certainly, for those who like to live with their heads in the clouds, it has everything they need. And Buddhism has an ethic which is unsurpassed.

Meanwhile China has managed perfectly well without any real religion at all, with Confucius coming up with a humanist ethic that needed no religion and with taoism providing everything those who want something 'spiritual' could wish for.

But all of this is a digression. Because the monotheistic God of Judaism, Christianity and Islam knows everything, he knows which of us will seek salvation and which of us will not. He knows who is destined for paradise and who is destined for hell. He knows the future as well as the present and the past. As Calvinistic Christians realised, this means that everything is predestined, fixed and unmoveable.

Belief in an all-knowing God destroys all our belief that we have freedom of will. It means that if I am predestined to be a 'slave to sin' nothing can change that – not the Law which I am predestined to disobey, nor the sacrifice of Jesus because I am predestined to have no faith in it. As Fraser would have put it in 'Dad's Army', I am doomed.

Belief in an all-knowing God – and after all God would not be God if he were not all-knowing – reduces us to the level of pre-planned machines. Freedom of will and freedom of choice or action are myths. God knows the future of each one of us and we have no power to alter that future. There is no escape.

In two verses, Paul has reminded us that God is all-knowing and has undermined everything that he has been arguing for. Belief in an all-knowing God leads to the most pessimistic conclusions that are possible but that pessimism is the perfectly logical outcome of that belief.

As I mentioned earlier, the Christian picture of God is rather more complicated than the simple belief that God is one and indivisible. They insist that they only worship one God but they go on to make this one God very complicated. They speak of the Trinity – three persons in one God.

When I was a student, some of my fellow students used to go to Hyde Park each weekend to speak about Christianity at Hyde Park Corner. One Sunday a very gifted and attractive student called Geoffrey Ainger was on the soap box when a heckler challenged him to define the Trinity. Off the cuff he replied:

'The Trinity, my dear fellow? Unity in community in perpetuity. . . Next question.'

Brilliant – but what did he mean?

To Christians, God is seen in the same terms as he is seen

by Jews and Moslems, but the Christian will perhaps focus as Jesus did on God as 'our Father', a rather more human, warm, loving kind of God than the other religions picture him. He is the first person of the Trinity.

To us, the word 'person' means an entity complete in itself. But when Christians speak of God as three persons, they are not speaking of three completely separate and distinct entities. They are speaking of one whole, just as three in one oil is one liquid. It is difficult for us to hold on to this idea of the unity of God when Christians go on to claim that Jesus is God.

God the Father – or God with parental attributes – causes no problems. Nor does God the Holy spirit, for we have often been told that 'God is a Spirit and those who worship him must worship him in spirit and in truth.' It is easy to see God as spirit and as having parental qualities – the same God. Only when we add Jesus to the mix do we find ourselves in trouble.

Paul was the only one of the apostles who had never known Jesus. He is not entirely consistent when he writes about him, but in the letter to the Colossians he spelt out his belief in Jesus as God more carefully and thoroughly than anywhere else. It is the first written attempt we have. The second was the wonderful first chapter of John's Gospel – which is much better known.

Paul said that 'Jesus is the image of the invisible God. His is the primacy over all created things.' 'In him everything in heaven and earth were created. The whole universe has been created through him and for him. He exists before everything and all things are held together in him.'

'He is the first to return from the dead.' (Which means that the Pharisees must have been wrong in their belief that obedience to the Law of God would lead to some kind of heaven after death.) According to Paul, Jesus was 'the first to return from the dead, to be in all things alone supreme. In him the complete being of God, by God's own choice, came to dwell.'

For many Christians the only possible reaction to these claims is one of worship and adoration. I can understand that reaction because for many years it was my own.

But it was a picture of Jesus which split the early church and led to a great deal of persecution, strife and death.

If Jesus really is God, then both Paul and John were right in claiming that he is eternal, from everlasting to everlasting, and fully involved in the work of God the Creator of all.

If we ignore all those Darwinian questions about creation then, so far so good. The real problems begin when Jesus becomes a man.

The claim is that Mary was impregnated without the co-operation of a man. She became pregnant by the Holy Spirit. This led to a baby being born, with all the normal frailties and dependence of a human baby and yet the human child was also God – and all this with no diminution in the powers of God over all.

Can a human child, helpless and ignorant and fully dependent on others, really be God? And if he can, will he not turn out to be a perfect human being?

The Christian claim is that he did. But a reasonably careful examination of the Gospels shows that, although he was undoubtedly a good man, he was not perfect. A perfect man would have treated his mother and siblings better and would have treated both Peter and Judas differently.

But the crucial questions emerge at the end of his life. He seems to have thought that he was offering himself as a pure and perfect sacrifice to God – the Son to the Father. This must make them independent of one another.

Again: if Jesus is God, God cannot die. So what happened on the cross? Certainly a man died. Had God slipped away from the body on the cross? Is this the meaning of Jesus' words 'My God, my God, why hast thou forsaken me?' Was the God-man no longer a duality? Or was God still alive in the dead body in the tomb?

And what of belief in the resurrection? Did God return to the body of Jesus, or was the God element in Jesus never dead? And now: Has the body of Jesus somehow become a part of the wholeness of God, Father, Spirit and Son?

The questions multiply and although they often sound pretty banal, they do need answering if we are to believe that it is possible for a real human being to be really and truly God as well. It was when I came to the conclusion that Jesus was not God that I first began to question the existence of any kind of divinity.

The claim that there is only one God is the pinnacle of all religious belief. Shared by Jews, Christians and Moslems, it is a matter of belief, not proof. Those who believe it usually commit themselves to one of those three religions. Those of us who do not, find that we can live our lives perfectly well without any kind of religion at all.

Earlier in this book, 1 claimed that Paul pointed us to three different paths of life. One was obedience to the law of God. One was faith in the saving power of the sacrifice of Jesus on the cross. The third has no need for a religion at all. Paul expressed it in one line of his letter to the Romans. At long last it is perhaps time that we had a look at this third path of life. For me, it is the only one that we need.

Chapter 10

Perseverance, Caulks and Glue

My first landlady when I was an adult was an elderly widow. Her husband had been the skipper of a 'dirty British coaster with a salt-caked smoke stack' (as John Masefield described such ships).

As with many elderly people, all the most ordinary things in our everyday lives were beginning to be a struggle for my landlady. Again and again, as she pottered around the house, I would hear her mutter 'perseverance, caulks and glue'. No doubt it was a phrase she had picked up from her husband.

It is also a summary of everything we need if we are to lead a decent life. We don't need God or gods. We don't need a rigid straightjacket of laws. We don't need someone else's sacrifice to earn us salvation, all we need is simple perseverance.

I claimed at the beginning of this book that most people want to live decent lives. I think that is true and what is more, I think that most of them achieve their aim. There are some – comparatively few – who choose otherwise. For whatever reasons, they choose to live bad, antisocial lives that lead to misery, pain, poverty, destitution and even death.

Because that is their choice there is nothing to be done with them except to lock them up and throw away the key, unless they come to the point where they choose otherwise. And heaven help all of us if they ever achieve positions of power. The evangelist will say that they need to be saved. That is perfectly true but what is also true is that nobody can be saved unless he actually chooses to change. Transformation does not come from outside us. It cones from within. Although we may be inspired by a Jesus-figure, transformation will only come if we choose to allow it to happen. And if we do so choose, we still have the ongoing task of learning to live well. For that, all we need is my landlady's perseverance.

Oddly enough, in spite of all that Paul has to say about Jewish law and Christian salvation, there is one brief moment where he recognises the truth of what I have just been saying. He would be horrified to hear me saying so in the way that I have. Because, if what I say is true, there was no need for a God to give his law to Moses; there was no need for a God to become a man and to sacrifice himself on a cross; there was no need for Jesus at all (which does not alter the fact that I value some of his teaching). In fact, if you follow this argument to its logical conclusion, you will discover that there is no need for God or gods at all.

So what do we need?

Don't just take my word for it when I say 'perseverance. Take Paul's word for it. Paul said that God would give 'glory, honour and immortality' to those whose lives were marked by 'steady persistence in well-doing.' 'For every well-doer there will be glory, honour and peace.'

Coming from Paul these words are absolutely incredible.

There is nothing about Jesus or his sacrifice on the cross:

nothing at all. Look at his words again. He said that we could ACHIEVE a relationship with God which brought all the usual rewards simply by living our lives well.

In point of fact I think that that is precisely what most religious people believe, whatever their religion may be. But it goes further than that. Forget about a relationship with God. Forget about the supposed rewards. What is it that most people, religious or not, think about the way they should live their lives?

Most of us don't actually think about it very much. We certainly don't try to put our thoughts into words. We simply get on with doing what we think we should do.

And what is that?

I reckon that most of the world's people live their lives as genuine, warm, kind, friendly people. That is the way their grandparents lived and that is the way their parents lived, and now that is the way they live. That is certainly my own experience of the people I've been dealing with all of my long life. In Paul's language they are well doers who persist in well doing – although they would probably be very surprised if you told them so.

They haven't needed a religion to make them this kind of person. And they certainly have not needed to have someone die cruelly on a cross as a sacrifice on their behalf.

They are not perfect. Of course they are not. None of us is. But they are good human beings.

If there is a God, that is all that is needed for them to be acceptable to him. And if there is no God they are living as humans should, and that is quite enough.

But please notice that it was Paul who set us off on this track. It was Paul who said that all that is expected of us is that we should be 'well-doers' 'persistent in well-doing.'

You may wonder why on earth I am making so much fuss about something so obvious.

It is because of all that we have come across in the opening chapters of this book – all the fuss that religious people make about something that is fundamentally so simple. If we want to live good lives, all that we need is perseverance or, in Paul's words, 'steady persistence in well-doing.'

Life really is as simple as that. The good life is as simple as that.

Well perhaps, not quite. What happens when things go wrong? What happens when we make a mess of our lives as many of us do? Sometimes many of us get things badly wrong. Unwillingly, unintentionally, we do a great deal of harm and damage or destroy many of our closest relationships. It is no use making a great fuss. The damage has been done. Sometimes we can put things right. Often we can't, but even where we can't, we can begin our own lives all over again. All that we need is those 'caulks and glue' – a decent repair kit.

Soon after the Second World War, one of my elder brothers suggested that we go and join a harvest camp. Harvest in those days required many labourers. It wasn't all done by huge machines. For us it involved a seventy mile cycle trip.

We had only gone about six miles when my brother had a puncture. It was then that I discovered that this admired veteran home from the army in Burma, neither knew how to mend a puncture nor even had a repair kit. I set to and used my own kit. While I did, he sat, watched, and ate both of our sandwiches.

By the time we had both finished we were able to continue with our journey.

So it is with life. If we get things badly wrong; if we have some sort of breakdown; if we make a proper mess of things; we just have to get out our repair kit, patch things up and make sure that they are air-tight or water-tight and then press on with our journey with that same perseverance or 'steady persistence in well-doing' that was needed in the first place.

Often we can do all the repairs ourselves. If we need help there are helpers around. Often, just a member of our family or a close friend but sometimes someone with special training – perhaps a counsellor or a psychiatrist. But ultimately life really is as simple as that. Patch things up as thoroughly as you can and start all over again.

When we get things badly wrong, we can't put everything right. We shall always remember and regret any harm we have done and any relationships we have spoiled. But, although the pain remains and perhaps the shame too, we find that we can genuinely 'start all over again' and with that simple element of perseverance, we can go on to lead a thoroughly good life.

Perhaps that is never harder than for someone who has become the slave of some kind of addiction: drink or drugs or gambling. Something in their make-up has dragged them down and it is desperately difficult to begin again. Many addicts never manage to break free even though they try. But even for those who do break free, the new road is one fraught with difficulty and hazard. The least little thing can throw them off course. I sometimes liken their journey to a game of 'Snakes and Ladders' without the ladders. Worse still, the dice only has a single dot on it. The recovering addict literally can only travel one step at a time, and the slightest false step will put him in the mouth of a snake and see him whizz right back to the beginning again.

Those of us who have never suffered addiction need immense understanding and patience if we are associated with a recovering addict, but we should also honour him and admire every step forward that he takes.

But still, ultimately and fundamentally, the message is the same. All that is needed for the good life gone wrong is 'caulks and glue' followed by endless perseverance – 'steady persistence in well-doing.'

Given these things, what will the good life look like: what are the elements which make up a good life?

Turn to any of the great teachers and you will find them coming up with similar things. Paul is no exception. From time to time he exhorts his readers to live their lives in a particular way. One of my favourite passages in his letters is to be found in the letter to the Philippians.

Paul suggested that we should give thanks for 'whatever has been true, whatever honourable, whatever has been just, whatever pure, whatever has been lovely, whatever gracious, whatever there has been of excellence, and anything worthy of praise.'

So living the good life involves a host of simple things like living honestly and with straightforward integrity, being kind and thoughtful in our relationships with other people and other creatures, showing patience and decency, and always doing our best no matter what we undertake. It means making the most of whatever abilities we have, not just for ourselves but for those on whom our lives impinge.

In other words, living a good life is extraordinarily ordinary, straightforward and down to earth. It needs no reward or punishments because it is its own reward. A good life will be a happy life, and that is true even if it proves to be a hard life marred by things outside our control, like long-term illness. All that is required of us is that we should do our best, whether for ourselves or for other people.

When I was a schoolboy, I had a headmaster who often seemed to have the most crack-brained ideas. Sometimes we simply had to endure them and sometimes we were able to persuade him to give them up or alter them. But I shall always honour him for one thing he did. When it came to school prize-giving day, he instituted one prize for 'perseverance and grit.' It seemed to me then, and has always seemed to me, to be the most valuable school prize of all. One of my closest school friends won it one year. He was later to need all of his perseverance and grit as a brain injury devastated and eventually shortened his life. But he battled on with all of his old spirit and good humour, leading a thoroughly worthwhile life as a farmer and a father. His wife and family showed the same qualities as he did.

Life is not necessarily easy, but the good life is both straightforward and simple. Any of us can live well if we so choose. With or without religion; with or without belief in gods; with or without the abilities that will take us to the top of the class or the head of some great institution; with or without the patience required to wade through a book such as this; the good life is within the grasp of every single one of us.

It is the only life worth living.

I find that I want to add a post-script to this chapter. Good and evil are not quite as black and white in their simplicity as I have suggested. As a school-boy I stole two books from a secondhand bookshop. Everyone will agree that what I did was wrong. But those two books, Wordsworth's and Tennyson's poems, have been of value to me throughout my life. There is no excuse for what I did. I can only hope that my life-long love of books and spending on books has redressed the balance. There are times when we do things that are wrong and when we damage and hurt other people. There is no avoiding the shame of that and it is worse still if we cannot put right the wrong.

Oddly enough, sometimes those wrongs we did will have been some of the most beautiful moments of our life. We shall neither forget them nor wish to deny them. They are a part of our own treasure even if they are also a part of our own pain. Good and evil are not quite as simple as we think – not quite as black and white.

But whatever the shade of colour of our past crimes, we can turn from them and begin again and strive to do better next time. Life is not a straightforward race. It is a hurdles race, and most if not all of us, will knock a hurdle over here and there and take a tumble ourselves. But we can always get up and carry on. And the wonderful thing is that we can all be winners after our own fashion.

All that the good life needs then is perseverance, caulks and glue.

d

Chapter11

A Matter of Choice

Our last chapter will have shown that the way we live is largely a matter of choice. That is even true for those wrestling with addiction of some kind. Most of our choices are fairly unthinking. They will always be influenced by such things as our health, our upbringing, our education, our economic situation; our appetites and our own range of abilities.

For example, my own range of abilities is so narrow that I could never have chosen to be any kind of man working in practical ways. I could never have been a carpenter, a builder, a plumber, an electrician, a mechanic – the list goes on. So, in all sorts of ways, our choices are limited.

But the fundamental choices remain. Paul suggested that we should choose to live in two basic ways. First, we should use whatever gifts we have to serve other people. He spoke of the 'spiritual gifts' we have and he seems to have had a fairly narrow concept of service.

Paul was right when he told us to respect one another's gifts. It is a pity that he was only interested in men and in gifts that are useful in worship. Where Paul went wrong was when he went on to try to evaluate those gifts and put them in a sort of descending order of usefulness and value. That ruins the whole thrust of this chapter.

Schools and the world of education make the same mistake when they value academic gifts above all others.

There are two things we need to take into account here. First of all, mutual respect demands that we respect people for who they are, not for what they can do. Respect for what they can do comes after respect for who they are. But respect for what they can do means respect for whatever they can do. There is no ascending or descending order of value in those abilities. There are some of us with practical gifts in say carpentry, building, roofing, plumbing, or mechanics. There are others of us who are a whizz at economics or administration and so on and so on. Although you can't put a value on these things, we do, with the result that some become rich and many remain poor. Proper respect for one another should mean that we are all treated alike, whatever our talents may happen to be. It would also involve the recognition that there are no gifts that are 'more spiritual' than any other.

Paul went on to say that none of our gifts have any value at all without love. That, taking in the whole field of the world of work, is perhaps a bit extreme, although loving what we do is extremely valuable and caring about those we do it with and for is also extremely important. But we are not going to quibble. Paul's emphasis on love went on to lead him into one of the finest expositions of love that you will ever come across – the passage used still in a host of marriage services.

Paul continued on the theme of love and the great value of it. 'If I have no love I am nothing.' All sorts of other things have their limitations and pass away but 'love never ends.'

He claimed that three things last for ever, 'faith, hope and love'. He was both right and wrong.

Those who have faith in God or in individual people can find their faith shattered or destroyed. The same is true of both hope and love. But it is also true – at least on the human level – that we can find our faith justified, our hopes fulfilled, and our love life-long. When these things are true life is wonderful indeed.

In the midst of all this from Paul there is a verse which has always saddened me:

'When I was a child, my speech, outlook, and my thoughts were all childish. When I grew up, I had finished with childish things.'

'What's wrong with that?' I hear you ask.

I find it desperately sad. Yes, we have to grow up. Yes, we have to start thinking and behaving like adults. But no, no, no, no! We should never, ever, 'finish with childish things' or cease to think like a child, appreciate like a child, lose a child's sense of wonder. I once saw a photo of a small girl looking at a flower. The sense of wonder and appreciation in that girl's face has lived with me ever since.

We lose a child's eye and a child's mind at our peril. We would do well to ensure that we never finish with childish things and with childish thoughts or a child's appreciation. These are amongst the most attractive gifts of all.

But just as Paul didn't seem to have much time for women, so he didn't seem to have much time for children, whoops: I have allowed myself to wander off course. We were talking about 'service' to others as one of the elements in a good life. The choice to serve is one which is ever present. The simple fact is that the whole of life involves us in service of one kind or another. Just being a husband or a

76

wife involves us in a lifetime of service as does being a parent. The fact that much of our service also earns us a living doesn't alter that at all. And the more we are able to take pride in our work, the more other people will benefit from it.

It doesn't matter a scrap what our talents are or what our job may happen to be. If we are living and working for the benefit of other people, that is service and it is one significant part of a good and decent life. In all that I have been saying, most people would have mentioned people like doctors, nurses and professional carers. Their service is obvious and means so much to us all. But we should not limit our conception of service to such obvious and highly valued areas of life. No matter how we live for others, we are living good and valuable lives.

In a host of different ways people choose to serve their fellows. And quite a lot of people are not content with the help they provide through their work. Many, many people go on to spend a good deal of their free time giving voluntary service through a host of different organisations; enriching the lives of the young, caring for the needy, looking after neglected animals and damaged birds – once again the list goes on and is endless.

Of course, I mentioned the most basic levels of service given by a multitude of us to our husbands or wives, or to our children. Service seems to be an almost universal feature of human life and mostly something we perform without so much as a passing thought. But it is such service that makes the wheels of life go round smoothly and freely.

All of our service depends on the kind of people we have

chosen to be. Turn to any of the great teachers and strip life down to its basics and you will always find them listing the kind of virtues they would expect from us. Paul was no exception.

Curiously enough, most of us nave never heard of many of these teachers. We may have heard of Abraham, the Buddha, Confucius, Moses, Jesus, or even some of the Greek philosophers like Plato, Epicurus or Aristotle, and we have probably heard of Muhammad. But even if we have heard of these ancient teachers or of more modern ones, very few of us have actually studied them or tried to find out what they taught or teach. If we have, we shall have discovered all sorts of similarities in their teaching and we shall find them looking for similar virtues in their followers. Paul was no exception. From tine to time in his letters he spoke of the qualities which should mark people living Christian lives. In the main, they are no different from the qualities we would expect to find in any decent life whether religious or not. They are the qualities I see again and again in the lives of those about whom I am asked to speak.

Very few of them are scholars. They know little or nothing of the things I have been speaking about in the earlier chapters of this book. Many of them have had no religious background to their lives of any significance. They have not been faultless or sinless or perfect any more than I have. They have mostly been comparatively unknown except in their own street or neighbourhood. But, without any serious thought, wisdom or background of teaching, they have lived good, decent, kind and loving lives. Within whatever scope was theirs, they have lived as well as they could and given the best they had. Not all that long ago I took the funeral of a man who had written a few poems. In one of them he wrote:

'I have hoped, I have planned, I have striven,
I have tried.
The best in me, I have given.'
(Tomas Stone)

There are masses of people who could write words similar to those. They have lived as well as they could and when their lives are complete, the rest of us honour them for all that they have been and for all that they have done.

From time to time Paul listed some of the virtues he expected from his followers. It makes a pleasant change from his usual rants about how awful we all are. He wrote such things as:

'Put on ... compassion, kindness, humility, gentleness, patience. Be forbearing and forgiving. To crown all there must be love and peace and gratitude.'

Or again, he says that Christian behaviour should involve 'love, joy, peace, patience, kindness, goodness, fidelity, gentleness and self-control.'

Mostly when he wrote like this, he set it all alongside rants about the kind of people we should *not* be and he tended to be much more vivid and expressive when he was ranting, but let me select one more set of quotes on the positive side:

'Speak the truth . . . work hard and honestly . . . be generous, and tender hearted and forgiving . . . Live for goodness, justice, truth . . . conduct yourselves like sensible men.' ('Men' notice. Paul rarely shows any sign of valuing or even considering women except to come down hard on them.)

I have already mentioned my favourite of all these selections from Paul from his letter to the Philippians, a challenge worthy of any of us:

'All that is true, all that is noble, all that is just and pure, all that is loveable and gracious, whatever is excellent and admirable – fill all your thoughts with these things.'

In making these selections I nave done my best to be generous to Paul and to pick out things that are positive in his letters. When you actually look at these things that he said, you will notice that they nave nothing in them which is necessarily religious. They have nothing to do with divine law or with religious salvation. They all have to do with living our ordinary lives as positively and well as we can.

Life, real life, is not about law, sacrifice, salvation and so on. It is not about the rewards and punishments of heaven or hell. We can forget about all those things. Life is about ordinary things like passion and service, determination and pluck. It is about endurance. For those of us who are lucky enough to lead long lives, the old song says it all:

'keep right on to the end of the road,
keep right on to the end.'

The rewards which come from making the right choices are immense. Many philosophers have spent a great deal of their time trying to work out the secret of happiness. There is no great secret. If we live well, striving for the kind of qualities Paul has spoken of, and trying always to do our best for other people, we shall be happy. Happiness is not something we have to strive for. It is a by-product of a good and decent life.

Ultimately life is not about complex, obscure philosophies, it is not about complicated and inexplicable religions. It is about simple things like 'doing your best.' It is not about God or gods. It is not about rewards and punishments. It is about playing the hand we have been dealt and playing it as well as we can. It is about simple things like human love and friendship; kindness, generosity and service.

And when, for whatever reason, things go wrong, it is about getting out the repair kit, mending things as best we can, and starting all over again. That phrase 'perseverance, caulks and glue' really does say it all. Life is about triumphs, failures, joys, sorrows; mending the breaks and redesigning. It is about recognising that the simpler we keep things, the better everything will be. Fundamentally, life is about ordinary goodness and decency and about ordinary love and service.

If we give our fellow men and women the respect they deserve and admiration for the way they have often beaten down adversity and come out smiling, we shall perhaps learn from them how to confront our own demons and beat down our own adversities so that we can live as well as they do.

If they help, then it may be worth turning to religions, philosophies, even books like this one, but more often than not, these will simply pass us by. We can live without them and most of us do. We can live WELL without them, and most of us do.

This has been a long and complex journey. I hope that it has not been too tedious. I have tried to pay proper respect where it has been due. But I have found once again that so much that was felt to be essential if we were to live well, brought up as I was in a Christian home, is absolutely irrelevant.

Life is so much simpler than I thought. It is ordinary. It is just a question of trying to get things right and sometimes getting them wrong. It is a question of choosing the right path and, if we get it wrong, retracing our steps and trying again. It is a question of helping one another, without ever claiming that we know better than the other. Hand in hand, we wander along life's pathway, trying to avoid the pot-holes and the muck, and laughing with and at one another at our clumsy attempts to avoid obstacles and walk straight on. Insofar as we follow that simple kind of pathway of virtue and service, we shall find that there is a great deal of laughter and real happiness – a depth of happiness which none of the awful tragedies of life can destroy, though they may dent it for a time.

I have been an exceptionally lucky man. I have had a very long and healthy life. I have got some things right and some things badly wrong. Curiously enough, I don't regret the things I have got wrong except for the hurt and damage they caused. There have been times when life has been a pretty desperate struggle but there has always been love – love given and love received – love and its less passionate partner, friendship. There has been perspiration, 'perseverance, caulks and glue' and there has been an immense amount of happiness and satisfaction.

I owe an immense debt of gratitude to a host of people, many of whom are now a part of that 'greater company' of those whose lives are ended. Soon it will be time for me to sign off. To my family and to my shrinking circle of friends, I would like to sign off with a sincere and warm thank you to you all.

Now where did I put my 'caulks and glue'?

The Discourse on Loving-Kindness

If you are wise and want to reach the state of peace,
you should behave like this:
You should be upright, responsible, gentle and humble.
You should be easily contented and need only a few things.
You should not always be busy.
You should have the right sort of work.
Your senses should be controlled and you should be modest.
You should not be exclusively attached to only a few people.
You should not do the slightest thing
that a wise person could blame you for.
You should always be thinking: May all beings be happy.
Whatever living beings there are, be they weak or strong,
big or small, large or slender, living nearby or far away,
those who have already been born
and those who have yet to be born,
May all beings without exception be happy.
You should not tell lies to each other.
Do not think that anyone anywhere is of no value.
Do not wish harm to anyone, not even when you are angry.
Just as a mother would protect
her only child at the risk of her own life,
So you should let the warmth of your heart go out to all beings.
Let your thoughts of love go through the whole world
with no ill-will and no hate.
Whether you are standing, walking, sitting or lying down,
So long as you are awake you should develop this mindfulness
This, they say, is the noblest way to live.
And if you do not fall into bad ways,
but live well and develop insight,
And are no longer attached to all the desires of the senses,
Then truly you will never need to be reborn in this world again.

(I wrote this so long ago that I have no idea how much it is my own
work and how much it comes directly from Buddhist sources.)